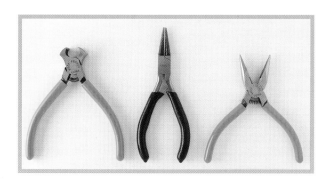

Basic Tools

Basic Findings

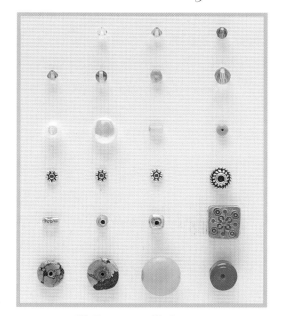

Basic Beads

Since wearing multiple earrings has come into style, take the trend further and wear three bracelets together. This trio of color-coordinated beads is gorgeous with any attire.

It's hard to believe that these incredible creations are made using pliers, wire cutters, common findings and a variety of beads. Crystals, bicones, and faceted beads give your jewelry the sparkle you want while pearls add that luscious shimmer. Silver spacers and natural stones give weight, body and richness to your unique design.

Once you begin this adventure, you won't want to stop. Look for Mary's companion books that feature necklaces and earrings as well!

Ocean Blues
see pages 6 - 7

Pinks & Pearls
see pages 8 - 9

Tibetan Colors
see page 14

Spring Fling
see page 15

Crystal Links
see pages 10 - 11

Tribal Colors
see pages 12 - 13

Earth, Sea & Sky
see pages 16 - 17

Turquoise & Crystal
see pages 18 - 19

Ocean Blues

Crimping the ends of jewelry wire and making wrapped loops are staple skills of jewelry making.

MATERIALS:
2 oval 5mm x 7mm fluorite beads (E)
5 Amethyst 5mm disks (G)
2 Aquamarine 10mm disks (X)
2 Green Swarovski 8mm round crystals (W)
3 Fluorite 10mm melon beads (K, L, M)
5 White 6mm pearls (Z)
5 Peridot 5mm disks (H)
1 round 15mm hill tribe bead (V)
2 Green Swarovski 6mm bicone crystals (F)
2 square 10mm coin pearls (Y)
1 square 5mm hill tribe spacer bead (R)
1 faceted 12mm x 16mm chalcedony bead (W)
5 Purple Swarovski 4mm bicone crystals (I)
1 Blue Swarovski 6mm crystal cube (O)

1 decorative 4mm x 7mm bali tube (P)
6 bali 4mm daisy spacers (S)
6 bali 6mm daisy spacers (T)
3 hill tribe 3 x 6mm square tube beads(Q)
8 Sterling 2" head pins (J)
4" of 22 gauge Sterling wire (C)
1 Sterling 6mm x 12mm lobster clasp(D)
3½" of Sterling chain (A)
2 Silver crimp beads (U)
10" of beading wire (B)
round-nose pliers
chain-nose pliers

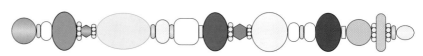

Thread beads on the beading wire as shown above.

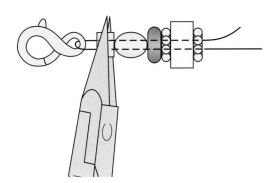

Thread one end of the wire through crimp tube, lobster clasp, then back through the crimp bead and a few beads of the bracelet. Flatten crimp with chain-nose pliers. Thread remaining beads onto wire.

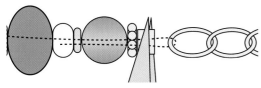

Thread a crimp bead on the end of beading wire. Pass the wire through the last link of chain, then back through the crimp bead and a few beads of the bracelet. Flatten the crimp bead with chain-nose pliers.

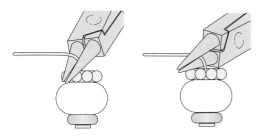

Thread an Amethyst disk, a small pearl and a small daisy spacer on a headpin.

Grasp the head pin with round-nose pliers touching the top of the spacer bead. Bend the wire at a 90° angle. Loosen your grip on the pliers and pivot them from horizontal to vertical.

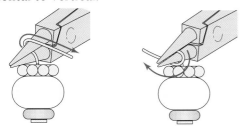

Wrap the end of the head pin over the top jaw of the pliers.

Reposition the wire on the bottom jaw of the pliers.

Wrap the wire around the bottom jaw of the pliers.

Slip the end of the head pin through the first link in the chain. Move the beaded portion of the bracelet and the chain out of the way and grasp the loop of the dangle with the pliers.

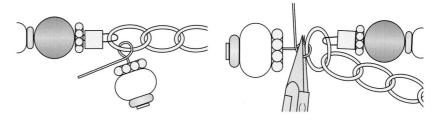

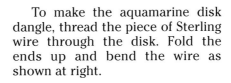

Without touching the beads on the pin, begin coiling the short end around the neck of the dangle. Begin the coils as close to the loop as possible. Make two or three coils, then clip the end of the wire close to the coils.

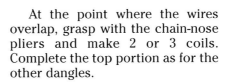

To make the aquamarine disk dangle, thread the piece of Sterling wire through the disk. Fold the ends up and bend the wire as shown at right.

At the point where the wires overlap, grasp with the chain-nose pliers and make 2 or 3 coils. Complete the top portion as for the other dangles.

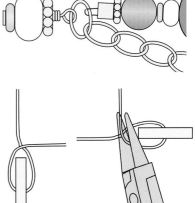

Referring to the illustration below for bead placement, attach the remaining dangles. Do not attach dangles to the last inch of chain - this portion of chain will be used to attach the lobster clasp.

Attach two dangles to the very last link to finish.

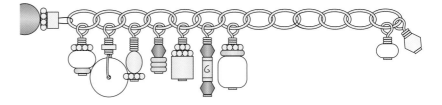

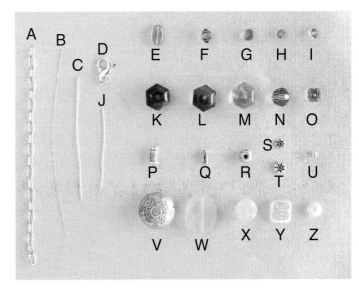

Pinks & Pearls

The cool luster of pearls and the shining sparkle of crystals combine to create a statement of elegance!

MATERIALS:
32" of 24 gauge Sterling wire (B)
9 coin pearls, round & square (D, F)
8 assorted Pink Swarovski
    4mm bicone crystals (A)
10 Sterling 6mm twisted jump rings (C)
1 Sterling 8mm x 12mm lobster clasp (E)
round-nose pliers

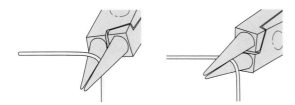

Cut a 4" long piece of 22 gauge wire. Grasp the wire with round-nose pliers about 1¼" from the top. Bend the wire at a 90° angle.

Loosen your grip on the pliers and pivot them from horizontal to vertical.

Wrap the short piece of wire over the top jaw of the pliers.

Reposition the wire on the bottom jaw of the pliers. Complete the loop by wrapping the short end of the wire around the bottom jaw of the pliers.

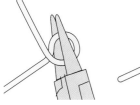 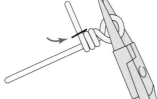

Remove the loop and hold it in place as shown at right. Without touching the long end of the wire, begin coiling the shorter piece of wire around the longer piece. Begin the coils as close to the loop as possible. Make two or three coils, then clip the end of wire close to the coils.

 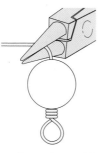

Thread on a pearl. Grasp the wire with your pliers about ⅛" from the end of the jaws. Bend the wire at a 90° angle.

Pivot the pliers from horizontal to vertical just as you did earlier.

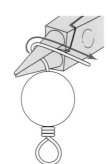 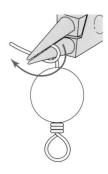

Wrap the wire around the top jaw of the pliers. Move the piece to the bottom jaw of the pliers to complete the loop.

Wrap this loop with 2 or 3 coils just as you did for the first loop.

Make wrapped loops on both ends of all the pearls.

To make the dangles, thread each crystal on a head pin and repeat the steps above.

We'll be using twisted jump rings to connect the pearl links and to hold the dangles in place. To open a jump ring, twist it to the side as shown at left.

Open a jump ring and thread on the clasp and one end of a pearl link as shown below. Close jump ring.

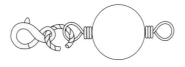

Open another jump ring and thread on the opposite end of the pearl link, 3 dangles, a square pearl link and three more dangles as shown below.

Close jump ring. Continue joining links with jump rings and crystals. Alternate square and round pearls. Complete the bracelet by attaching the last link to the closed loop of the clasp. You won't add crystal dangles to this connection.

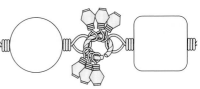

Use the techniques you learned while making this bracelet to make matching earrings. Just thread dangles on two jump rings and then attach the rings to posts or fishhook ear wires.

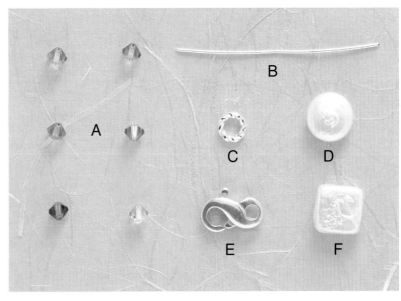

Crystal Links

This delicate looking yet sturdy bracelet is a quick project!

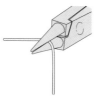

MATERIALS:
17" of fine Sterling chain (G)
20 Swarovski 4mm crystals:
    4 each Jonquil, Rose, Fuchsia,
    Light Peach, Colorado Topaz (F)
2 Sterling 4mm x 6mm cones (C)
48" of 24 gauge Sterling wire (A)
3 Bali three strand connectors (B)
6mm x 10mm Sterling lobster clasp (D)
6mm Sterling closed ring (E)
round-nose pliers

Cut six 1¼" pieces and six 1½" pieces of chain using wire cutters or an old nail clipper. Next, cut a 4" long piece of Sterling wire. Grasp the wire with round-nose pliers about 1¼" from the top. Bend the wire at a 90° angle.

Loosen your grip on the pliers and pivot them from horizontal to vertical.
Wrap the short piece of wire over the top jaw of the pliers.
Reposition the wire on the bottom jaw of the pliers. Complete the loop by wrapping the short end of the wire around the bottom jaw of the pliers.

Remove the loop and thread on the end link of a 1½" piece of chain. Hold the loop in place as shown below.

Without touching the long end of the wire, begin coiling the shorter piece of wire around the longer piece. Begin coils as close to the loop as possible. Make two or three coils, then clip the end of wire close to the coils.

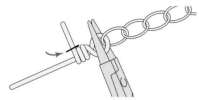

Thread on a crystal, a 3 strand silver connector and another crystal. Grasp the wire with the pliers about ⅛" from the end of the jaws. Bend the wire at a 90° angle.
Pivot the pliers from horizontal to vertical just as you did earlier.

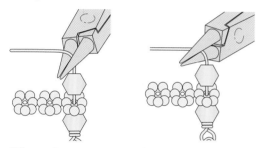

Wrap the wire around the top jaw of the pliers. Move the piece to the bottom jaw of the pliers and wrap the wire around the bottom jaw of pliers.

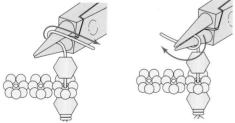

Thread on the last link in another 1¼" piece of chain. Wrap this loop just as you did earlier.

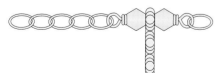

Repeat the steps above for the other two spaces in the connector.

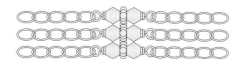

Make a loop in another 4" piece of wire. Before wrapping the loop, thread on one of the chains from the center section. Wrap as before. Wrap as before. Thread on a crystal, the top loop of a connector and another crystal. Before wrapping the loop, thread on the last link in a 1½" piece of chain. Repeat for the other two chains of the section. Work the opposite side of the center spacer in the same manner.

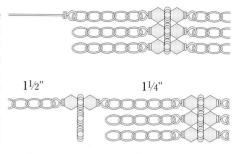

1½"   1¼"

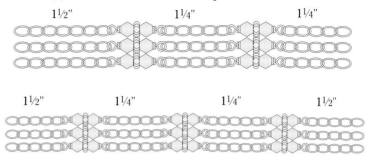

1½"   1¼"   1¼"

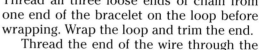

1½"   1¼"   1¼"   1½"

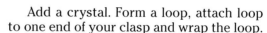
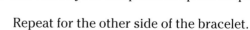

IMPORTANT!

These instructions will make an 8" bracelet. Measure your wrist. Next, measure your bracelet. Include 1" for the length of the clasp. If your bracelet will be too large, trim a few links of chain from each of the 1½" sections to make it fit.

Make a loop in another 4" piece of wire. Thread all three loose ends of chain from one end of the bracelet on the loop before wrapping. Wrap the loop and trim the end.
Thread the end of the wire through the large end of a cone.

Add a crystal. Form a loop, attach loop to one end of your clasp and wrap the loop.

Repeat for the other side of the bracelet.

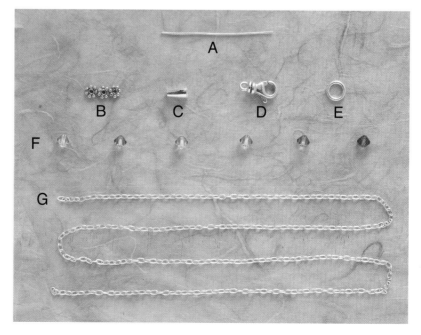

Tribal Colors

Show your love of nature's creations with swirl coral, silver, turquoise and jade around your wrist! Chain links make the length adjustable.

MATERIALS:
6 Coral 8mm x 10mm beads (D)
5 Turquoise 12mm disks (G)
6 Turquoise 5mm disks (A)
2 Olive jade flat 12mm rectangles(E)
3 Olive jade 4mm x 6mm tubes (B)
3 hill tribe 5mm square
   tube spacers (K)
2 square hill tribe 10mm
   spacers (N)
2 hill tribe 3mm x 6mm
   triangle spacers (M)
3 8mm pearls (C)
2 Silver 6mm daisy spacers (J)
Silver 3mm daisy spacers (I)

1 hill tribe 12mm
   diamond bead (Q)
2 Sterling 6mm bead caps (L)
1 Sterling 8mm bead cap (O)
5 Sterling 2" head pins (R)
4" of 22 gauge Sterling wire (U)
1 Sterling 8mm x 12mm
   lobster clasp (P)
2 Silver crimp beads (H)
12" of beading wire (T)
2" of Sterling chain (R)
round-nose pliers
chain-nose pliers

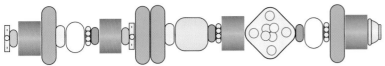

Thread beads on the beading wire as shown above.

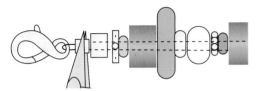

Thread one end of the wire through a crimp tube, the lobster clasp and then back through the crimp bead plus a few beads of the bracelet. Flatten the crimp with the chain-nose pliers. Trim excess wire.

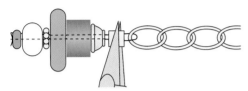

Thread a crimp bead on the remaining end of beading wire. Pass the wire through the last link of chain, then back through the crimp bead and a few beads of the bracelet. Flatten the crimp bead with chain-nose pliers. Trim excess wire.

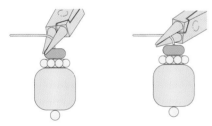

Thread an Olive jade rectangle, a medium bali spacer and a small Turquoise disk on a head pin.

Grasp the head pin with round-nose pliers touching the top of the Turquoise bead. Bend the wire at a 90° angle. Loosen your grip on the pliers and pivot them from horizontal to vertical. Wrap the end of the pin over the top jaw of the pliers.

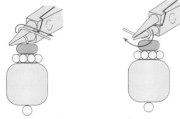

Reposition the wire on the bottom jaw of the pliers.

Wrap the wire around the bottom jaw of the pliers.

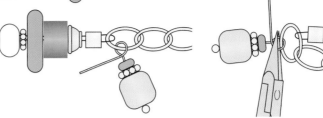

Slip the end of the head pin through the first link in the chain. Move the beaded portion of the bracelet and the chain out of the way and grasp the loop of the dangle with the pliers.

Without touching the beads on the head pin, begin coiling the short end around the neck of the dangle. Begin the coils as close to the loop as possible. Make two or three coils, then clip the end of the wire close to the coils.

To make the Turquoise disk dangle, thread the piece of Sterling wire through the disk. Fold the ends up and bend the wire as shown at right.

At the point where the wires overlap, grasp with the chain-nose pliers and make 2 or 3 coils. Complete the top portion as for the other dangles.

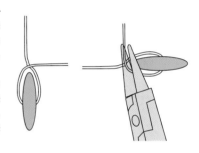

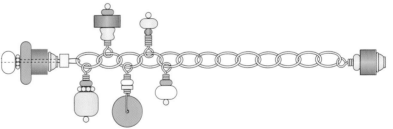

Referring to the illustration above for bead placement, attach the remaining dangles. Do not attach dangles to the last inch of chain - this portion of chain will be used to attach the lobster clasp.

Attach a dangle to the very last link to finish.

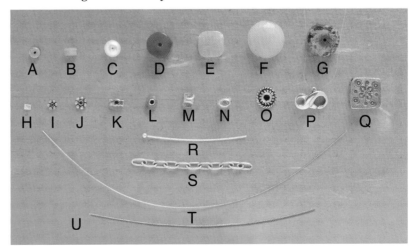

Thread beads on the jewelry wire as shown below, near the bottom of the page.

Adjust the number of beads to make the bracelet fit your wrist, allowing 1" for clasp.

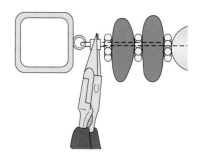

Thread one end of the wire through a crimp tube. Pass the wire through one end of the toggle clasp and then back through the crimp bead and a few beads of the bracelet. Flatten the crimp with the chain-nose pliers.

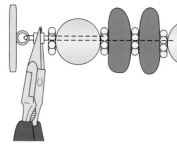

Thread another crimp bead on the remaining end of jewelry wire. Pass the wire through the other half of the toggle clasp and then back through the crimp bead and a few beads of the bracelet.

Flatten the crimp bead with the chain-nose pliers.

Tibetan Colors

Take an imaginary journey to a land of ancient civilizations, soaring mountains and brilliant colors while you make this ethnic bracelet!

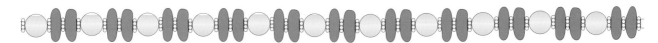

MATERIALS:
22 Turquoise 10mm disks (F)
11 round 4mm amber beads (D)
34 Silver 4mm daisy spacers (B)
2 crimp tubes (A)
1 Silver 12mm toggle clasp (C)
12" of beading wire (E)
chain-nose pliers

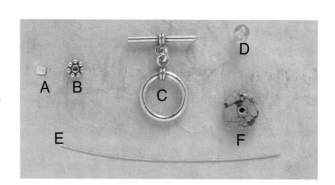

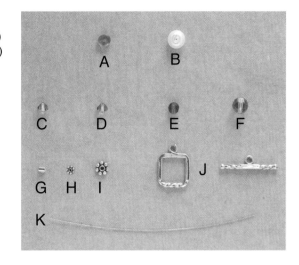

MATERIALS:
22 White 6mm pearls (B)
3 Swarovski 6mm Rose crystal rounds (E)
4 Swarovski 4mm Rose crystal rounds (D)
3 Swarovski 4mm Fuchsia crystal
   bicones (C)
14 Silver 3mm daisy spacers (I)
6 Silver 5mm daisy spacers (H)
11 peridot 5mm disks (A)
2 crimp tubes (G)
1 Sterling 12mm square toggle clasp (J)
12" of beading wire (K)
chain-nose pliers

Thread beads on the jewelry wire as shown above, at the top of the page.

(Add additional beads to one end if you need to make the bracelet larger, allowing 1" for clasp.)

Spring Fling

Circle your wrist with the refreshing colors of spring!

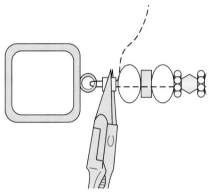

Thread one end of wire through a crimp tube. Pass the wire through one end of the toggle clasp, then back through the crimp bead. Flatten the crimp with chain-nose pliers. Trim the excess wire.

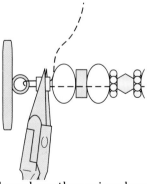

Thread another crimp bead on the remaining end of jewelry wire. Pass the wire through the other half of the toggle clasp and then back through the crimp bead. Flatten the crimp bead with chain-nose pliers. Trim excess wire.

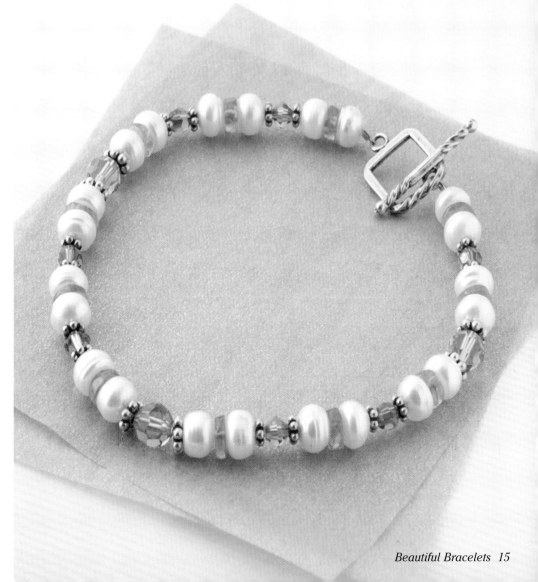

Earth, Sea & Sky

*Learning to crimp the ends
of jewelry wire is a basic skill.*

MATERIALS:

9 Turquoise 8mm disks (Q)
4 Turquoise 12mm disks (R)
6 Silver 3mm daisy spacers (B)
5 Silver 5mm daisy spacers (C)
6 Silver 10mm daisy spacers (J)
2 triangular 6mm hill tribe
  beads (E)
1 square 6mm hill tribe bead (F)
2 bali 7mm bead caps (H)
2 bali 7mm thick spacers (I)
2 bali 5mm thick spacers (D)
1 hill tribe 3mm x 6mm
  vertical tube bead (G)
1 Swarovski 8mm crystal
  round (N)
1 Fluorite 10mm melon bead (O)

4 Aquamarine 10mm disks (P)
1 Swarovski 6mm cube (M)
3 Swarovski 10mm pearls (T)
1 6mm pearl (S)
2 crimp tubes (A)
1 Sterling 8mm x 12mm
  lobster clasp (L)
1 Sterling 8mm closed ring (K)
beading wire (U)
chain-nose pliers

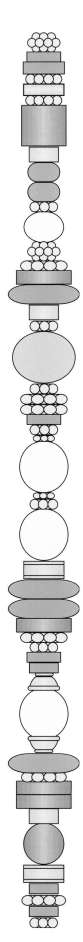

How the bracelet is made

String all the components of the bracelet on beading wire and crimp the ends to a clasp.

Let's Begin

Thread beads on the wire as shown in the illustration on the left.

Adjust the number of beads to make the bracelet fit your wrist.

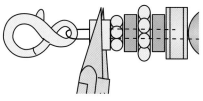

Thread one end of the wire through a crimp tube. Pass the wire through one end of the lobster clasp and then back through the crimp bead and a few beads of the bracelet. Flatten the crimp with the chain-nose pliers.

Trim the excess wire.

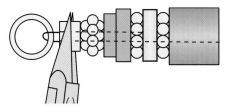

Thread another crimp bead on the remaining end of jewelry wire. Pass the wire through the closed ring and then back through the crimp bead and a few beads of the bracelet. Flatten the crimp bead with chain-nose pliers.

Trim the excess wire.

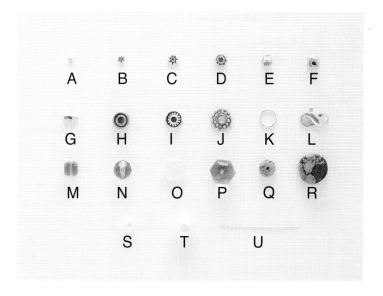

Turquoise & Crystal Bracelet

Austrian crystals provide sparkling accents when scattered among turquoise tubes the colors of earth and sky!